Poems

ISBN-13: 978-84-944559-0-2
Real House Publishing SL, 2018

An Accidental Visit

Catalina Lira

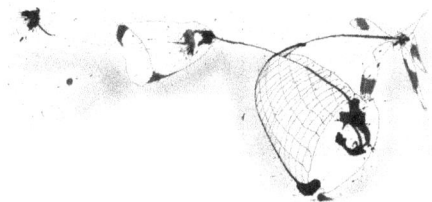

The walk along the street of your words

You were worthy of love ...

The different streets exist in towns.
But I would like to find the street
which was full of your sunny words.
I remember it was summer.
I remember it was the town.
The town was a ruler of various streets.
crowded streets...
deserted streets...
dead-end streets...
I preferred the unusual street of your words
which you created for me specially.
Nobody else knew my secret.
I have found the town.
I have found the street.
I have a walk along the street of your words.
They did not disappear after a long time.
My walk is full of your sunny words.
I know them all except
the words "He was worthy of love".
These new words are written
by a sad drizzling rain
on a glass of pools
for me specially.

An accidental visit

The visitor was none other than the king.
He did not know that he was such a mighty person.

I did not realize it at that time either.
But the visitor was the king.

The king knew only two languages.

The first was the language of plants.
The second was the language of clouds.

At that time, I knew the language of the sea.
At that time, I spoke in the language of the rain.

We did not recognize that clouds and rains
have very similar languages.

Therefore, we could have a deep understanding of each other.

The king left my home because it was an accidental visit.
The rose that he brought me was rooted in the garden soon.

However, I do not understand its fragrant words.
The king saved the key to his language for himself only

because he was a lone proud king.

Wind and Silence

One day the Wind has made friends with the Silence.
The Silence was taciturn and tranquil.
The Silence was so different from the Wind
that the Wind was admiring it.

They were walking together along the endless fields.
The Wind was lifting the Silence up in the sky.
And they were flying above the surprised Sea.

Because the Sea knew that
if the Wind flies in the air then
the Silence could not be there.
The Sea knew that
if the Silence is in the sky then
the Wind has not a chance to be there.

But the friendship can unite the contraries
and to make a connection of the contrasts.

Different steps

The steps of rain are painted by bright new flowers.
The steps of rain are like music on my window.
Rain is the great composer of nature.

But I listen to the rainy steps of my age by every new year.
I hate this music of steps of cold time
that never listen to my coloured soul.

Please, tell me…

My dear, please tell me about a beautiful future.
My dear, please tell me about the fulfilment of my hopes.
My dear, please tell me about wonderful days.

I understand that the most of your words are falsehoods.

Please, do not worry. I will not analyse them.
I need some rest with help of your words
that are coloured of your love for me.

The result

Many drops created a heavy rain.
Many stones created a big castle.
Many words created a new story.

What will be the result by us, people?

The gifts of the wind

My old friend the wind had flown into my room.
It had been flying many years for our meeting
Since the days of my childhood.

The wind wanted to bring my happy childish dreams to me.
The wind hoped to add some gladness to my present life.
It had put its beautiful gifts on the table in my room.

There have been colourful flowers, leaves, a smell of a garden
and a few cold drops of transparent rains.

I have taken flowers in my hands…
I have taken leaves in my hands…
I have felt a kiss of the cold drops of the rains on my skin.
I smiled.

But I could not take the smell of a garden in my hands.
"It looks like my childish dreams," I told the wind sadly.

The city and the moon

It was winter and the full moon.
I was walking with my little son in the evening city.

The city was full of busy people.
The cars were hurrying along the big prospect.
The windows of the big shops were illuminated brightly.
It was winter and the busy city.

Suddenly my son told me seriously,
"The city and the moon are utter strangers.
They do not notice each other."

It was winter and the full moon.

Please, do not destroy air-castles

The child has built a wonderful castle by sand.
Please, do not tell him about the disappearance
of his castle by rain.

The girl has built a wonderful castle of her dream.
Please, do not tell her about the fragility of her dream by life.

The man has built a wonderful castle of his transparent hope.
Please, do not destroy his belief to the future.

Do you know that he will be right if
nobody tells him about the weakness of his hope now?

The words

I wanted to express various emotions with my words.

I complained to you about the problem with it,
"It is difficult to find correct words for the feelings."

"You may not place a big lake in a vase,"

You found words of sense with a short answer.

A strong rain

A strong rain walks behind the windows of my house.

Sometimes he knocks at the glass of the windows.

Maybe he wants to enter the house...

Perhaps it is an interesting feeling to be a friend of the rain.

He could tell me how he came from the sky
to the door of my house.
He could tell me the stories of his different loves to the stars.
He could tell me many unusual stories of the sky.

A strong rain walks behind the windows of my house.

Let him come in …

What time is it?

You have asked me, "What time is it?"

"It is the time of the middle of the day
when butterflies fly above the yellow flowers."

You have told me, "No. Please, tell me.
What time is it?"

"It is the time of your yearning about
many days of your past loneliness."

"No, dear woman. Now it is the time of my happiness
because I have touched time by your tender lips,"
you answered the question yourself.

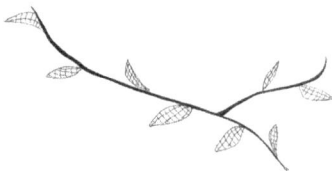

Wings

I want to take time in my hands.
I would like to understand what it is.

My friend tells me, "Please, take your watch
in your hands.
You will see the moving of time."

But I want to take time in my hands.
I wish to understand the emotions of it.

My friend tells me, "Please, take water of the river
in your hands.
You will have a piece of running time."

But I want to take time in my hands.
Can I realize this wonderful feeling?

My friend tells me,
"You may take time in your hands if you fly in the sky.
But you will not have hands at that time.

Maybe you will have two wings.
So time will fly on your wings with you."

Secure retreat

Wind took my hat.
It was blown away.
I felt a cold touch of the rain on my face.

Newspapers brought dirt into my soul.
TV reports built dark walls of hatred.

I opened the door of my home.
You opened your arms for me.
The circle of your embrace
shut out the madness of the world for me.

Wind

Wind was walking along the paths of the green field.
I wanted to see this walk but it could not be possible.

Only flowers and grass were showing the way of the wind.
They were rustling along the pathway of its soft steps.

I asked the wind to make me its companion.
The wind laughed at my words.

"You should be a cloud for that," the wind whispered to me,
"I do not need people as friends."

As your love for me…

You had presented an amazing flower to me.
I had decided to understand where beauty of the flower lived.

I had divided the flower into different parts.
I had taken the yellow petals in my hands.
I had taken the green leaves in my hands too.

But it was not the soul of beauty.

The wind blew it all off from the table
where I had put the leaves and tender yellow petals.

I did not recognize how beauty of the flower was made.

As your love which I separated into parts for my studying
this disabled flower did not exist any-more anywhere.

As your love for me…

Beautiful gifts

What did you bring to me, my unknown guest?
What did you put in the basket
which is on the door-step now?
Why did you go away without meeting me?

I have opened the basket with interest.
Oh! Many books and a ray of the sun…
Oh! Many beautiful recollections
and the music of the sea…
Oh! Many coloured words of love
and the perfume of a rainy day…

I look at the road of a big garden.
You are standing with a big bouquet of flowers.

Thank you.

You are not mistaken with your beautiful gifts in the basket.

The language of people

If I want to understand the talk of trees
then I should speak their language.

(I am sure they have interesting talks.)

If I want to understand the emotions of the sea
then I should know its words.

(I am sure the sea has a wise soul.)

If I want to recognize the rustling phrases of grass
then I should know its green tender language.

But I know the language of people.

It is the language
which hides true emotions and thoughts.

Often I think that I do not understand
this cold language either.

Recollection

On that day the huge sea was playing with strong waves.
Hot sand of the coast...
We were walking along a coast of the deep sea.

You flung your hat in the air.
Suddenly the wind caught your hat and put it above
a big wave.
The wave has brought the hat back to my feet.

"I would like to be this wave," you told me seriously.

A special evening

It was a special evening.
Sometimes nature offers it to people.

Feelings were dancing in the air.
They created a space of tenderness.

Motes were dancing in the sunbeam.
Shadows were dancing on the grass.
Blossoms were falling from the trees.

But you danced your chance away
to tell me about your love for me.

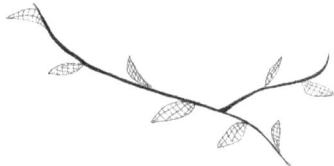

Music of stones

"I love you," the man cried to the woman.
The wind put the words on its wings and flew away.

"I love you," the man cried to the woman again.
The echo returned all words to him.

She did not love him more.

He saw how she was going away along a transparent
road of love.

Clouds were her companions.
She had a bouquet of flowers in her hands.

The echo of her lost love to him was playing
music of stones under her feet.

A connection

A connection between
the sky and the earth
is the rain.

A connection between
a writer and people
is a book.

A connection between
you and me
is a night dream.

You do not ask my permission to come
inside a transparent space of visible feelings.

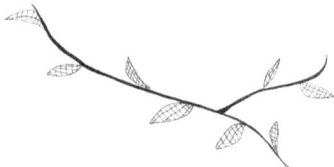

Night city of night steps

Many lone persons walk in a strange night city
of a warm night.
It is a city of night steps.
Every person has a little night in their soul.
Every person listens to the music of the high black sky.

So much freedom…

It is a calm city of night steps.
Drops of rain make their wet steps in the streets
of the city too.
It is a time of deep thoughts.
It is the city of reflection of time.

Night city of night steps…

I was deathless at that time

I did not know about death
when I was a little girl.
Nobody had told me about it at that time.
I was sure all was eternity
although I did not know
the deep meaning of this word too.

I did not know about death.
So I was a deathless girl at that time.

My beloved grandmother showed me
the existence of the space of death.
She went inside that space.

She never come back to me
although I waited for her every day.
I was sure my grandmother would come back to me
if she could find a possibility to do so.

…

She did not come back.
So I felt the stern cold of the breath of death.

People are dancing…

Music was the true friend of Eternity.
It was an important friendship
that was created by the Sky.
They never had a quarrel until the Dance came.

The Dance is the servant of people.

Music has mixed its emotions with the Dance.
People are dancing…

Eternity observes them attentively.

True interest

I had wanted to have a talk with my friend.
My friend did not understand my words.

I had wanted to express my feelings to the night wind.
It took my feelings and laughed at them.

I had wanted to add my thoughts
to the huge picture of the world.

The world went away into a new day
with a plenty indifferent people in it.

I sat down on the old bench under the big green tree.
And a little bird looked at me with true interest.

I remember...

"I remember I was a bird in my previous life,"
an old woman told her husband.
"It is not possible, my dear," the man answered her,
"You could be only a woman."

"I remember I was a butterfly in my previous life,"
a black bird told her mother.
"It is not possible, my child," the mother answered her,
 "You could only be a bird."

"I remember I was the rain," a white cloud told the sky.
"All is possible here, my dear cloud," the sky replied
and it kissed the cloud with a bright ray of the sun.

Love

Nobody knows perfectly what love is.

But the word 'love' is alive.

People tell this word to each other.

Pronounced word touches the space of real love.

Then some rays of that huge light space are sent to people

with the short word 'love'.

Sometimes

Sometimes I would like to take my favourite fish
in my hands out of the aquarium.
I could kiss the fish and pat it on its head.
But I can't do it in spite of my wish
because I understand what would happen.

Sometimes I would like
to tell you, my beloved man...
Please, do not attempt to take me from my art space
because it is a strange space which is necessary for me
like water is necessary for the fish.

White book

It was a white book without words.
It was the book of eternal sense.

I walked along the pages of the book.
Perhaps my steps wrote the story of my life.

So the white book was transformed into
                                        shadows,
echo and recollections.

Travellers

We study to travel in life.
We study to travel in the light.

There is a large space of love for us.
There is a large space of death in the night.

We are travellers from world to world.
We are travellers from dream to dream.

We need a simple thing.
We need a space of beginning.

All the emotions of our trip
are the emotions of different lives.

We remind the travellers as dreams
which were made of an incredible light.

About love

You asked me why I have only a few poems
about love.
"It is such an important feeling…" You told me.

I know, my dear.

But I know what love is.
Therefore, I sense the futility of the words
before the brightness of this feeling.

The question

What do people want to find on other planets?
New love or new life or new place for different wars…

What do you wish to find in my soul?
New love or new life or new place for spiritual wars…

The only thing

I have knitted a jumper by your warm words.
I wear it in the winter days of my fate.
Your words give me warmth in cold days
because I am inside them by my jumper.

You ask me to knit something for you.
Fresh wind will be created by my words.
I am sorry. But it is the only thing
that can be knit by my words about you.

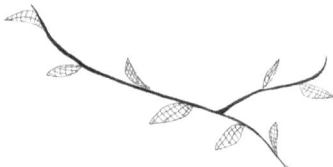

Where are you going?

"Where are you going?"
People asked a little boy who was running
along the road in a field.

"I want to catch this beautiful butterfly!"
The boy cried to them.

"Where are you going?"
People asked a strong, handsome man
who was striding along a street at night.

"I need to find the most beautiful woman in this world.
I did not find her in the daytime.
Maybe fantastic time of night clouds will help me."
The man answered people.

"Where are you going?"
People asked the old man who was sitting
and looking at the stars near the huge sea.

"I do not know, my dears.
I hope to find the answer of this question too."

The old man told them with sadness.

Your way

You were like a strong free river.
I could not catch you like a free animal neither.
I put my hands into the water.
I was sure I touched your soul.
But the water was moving constantly.
And the big clouds were moving with water reflection.

You were like a big strong river.
I was sitting on the bank of your moving soul.
I put a little leaf above the water.
It swam away with the water.
It was a traveller which did not wish to catch you.

The leaf accepted your way and
You accepted the leaf.

Soul and body

Different souls walk in this world.
Souls are dressed in bodies
so that nobody could see the souls naked.

Coloured souls cannot be mixed with each other.

It is a lone walk along the road of life.
People mix their bodies.
It is easy.
It gives the hope of understanding.

But lone souls walk in the world.

Different impressions

I looked at the tree.
I saw the image of a strong person
whose hands were outstretched branches to the sky.

My husband looked at the tree.
He saw the big marquee of green leaves
where we could have coolness in that hot day.

My son looked at the tree and cried,
"It is a lofty tower! I will climb up this tower now."

You

I created the planet of my dreams.
I liked to walk along the roads of words.
The sea was full of the rays of the sun.
Do you know what the sun was on my planet?
It was a secret for all people too.
I lay on the green grass of my poems.
Clouds painted beautiful stories in the sky.
It was a perfect planet without people on it.

Do you know how I was surprised
when I met You on my planet one usual day?

Because I had forgotten
that I had created your image in my dream too.

Time

Time decided to become free.
Time had the wings made of the light of the stars.
Time was flying over the various cities.
It hoped to become free
from desire of people to have an orderly time.

Time knew that its soul was different and free.
Time knew that its soul was expressed with various colors.
Time was looking for people who did not need time.
So Time could be free from all people.

Maybe the lovers did not notice time.
No.
Maybe children …
No.
Maybe old people because of their wisdom…
No.

 Cities, cities, cities…

The tired Time was flying with help of its wings
made of the light of the stars.
People were sleeping.
«Do you feel a freedom in my night city?»
The Night asked Time.
And Time felt the touch of freedom to its tired soul..
But the night sleep of people is so similar to the death.
And Time understood that it is not possible
to be free from people.

The leaf and the wind

"I am free.
I fly above trees.
I am strong.
I fly among the birds,"
the leaf sang its happy words.

The wind was smiling to its assured song,
"I am like the father for this little leaf."

If I could be

If I could be a flower
then I would be glad to have a friend
such as morning dew.

If I could be a bird
then I would like to have a friend
such as a fresh breeze.

If I could be a cloud
then I would be happy
to be friends with the sky.

But I am a woman.

I wish to have a friendship with you,
my beloved serious man.

Together

May I paint a beautiful day for you?

I want to paint you a day in which you will be happy.
What should I take for my picture?
What colours do you prefer, my beautiful man?
May I paint the picture of love for you?

I will mix the perfume of the rainy summer day
with some rays of the sun.

I will put some green leaves on the canvas of the picture.
My picture will have the painted sky and the music of my laugh.
The birds will fly in the sky.
Nobody can catch them.

May I paint the beautiful day for you?
I am the painter. My profession is a wonder.
It will be the most beautiful picture that I ever created.
You will walk with me along the painted sea of my picture.

Visible breath

The breath of the earth becomes visible breath
by the tender green grass of the field.

The breath of the sky becomes visible breath
by the light summer rain.

The breath of your love to me became visible breath
by our little baby.

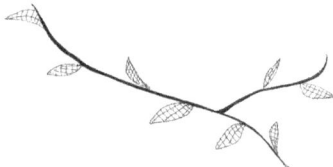

A strange city

It is an empty city. There are no people in it.
There are many different feelings living in the city
such as Love and Gladness, Sadness and Solitude.

They leave their strange transparent houses every morning.
They tell each other, "Good morning."
They even have a friendship with each other.

It is a strange thing
But Love prefers to be friends with Sadness.
And Gladness has a friendship with Hope.

Only Solitude does not want to have a friendship with anybody.
Solitude goes to the border of this strange city.
Solitude sits down on the huge stone near the sea and looks far.

The key

Your love is like a warm plaid.
I can be protected with it in cold evening.

Your love is like a tender song.
It affords consolation to me if I am sad.

I like the invisible space of your love
where I feel so much comfort.

Nobody can open this space because
the key to this space is my love to you.

A statue of feeling

The long shadow of the night song of the sea kissed the coast.
The sun returned to the sky after a short summer night.
The birds began their morning concert.

Only a man and a woman were sitting near each other
on the coast without moving.
There were like a statue created of love.

And it was not important for them that their lives and love
would be forgotten with the cold time of centuries.

The river

A river was going to the space of huge water.
The river had heard the birds say
that the sea was not far.

The unusual character and deep emotions
of the river were famous

among trees
and birds
and flowers.

It was a very strong and proud and deep river.

The sea opened its embraces for the river.
It was the place of the endless water
that the river saw in its dream.
Many drops of the sea were like a crowd of people.
The river became similar to a plenty of drops in the sea.

It was a very strong and proud and deep river …

The walk
along the border of the sky

Who can walk
along the border of the sky?

It is Rain.

It takes a big gray umbrella.
Its steps play music of drops.
Rain goes indifferently.

A small cloud sits on its shoulder
like a white furry cat.

The sky is a usual long wet road
under the feet of the sad Rain.

The small green Boat

I am in a small green boat which drifts along the
river of my fate.

Is it day-time?

Many birds are on the board of the boat.
They can fly but they look at the banks of the river
as the different captains of one boat.

Is it night-time?

I want to ask the star in the sky to make my way.
All the birds will fly away in the sky.
The only star will be the captain of my fate.

Your recollections

I did not give you a flower
that you could put among the sheets of an old book.
So you wanted to save a piece of my feeling for you.

I did not give you a small bottle of my favourite perfume
that you could feel my aroma although I would be far from you.

I did not give you my photo
because I will be another person in a few years.

But you will always have a space of your recollections about me
where you can meet me unchanged.

I will have a bouquet of flowers in my hands.
That bouquet will have the aroma of my favourite perfume.

The circles of life

The circles of our life.

Winter,
Spring,
Summer,
Autumn,
Winter.

Leaves of a big tree of life lie on water.

Winter, Spring, Summer, Autumn, Winter.

The moon swims in the sky.
Leaves swim on the circles of water.

Winter,
Spring,
Summer,
Autumn,
Winter.
We are like leaves inside the circles of life.

Expected meeting

Eternity hoped to have a meeting with Love.
Love promised to come to the night sea.
Eternity was waiting for Love for many minutes
after the sun went away to sleep.
Eternity was waiting for Love for many days.
Eternity was waiting for Love for many years.

Minutes...
Days...
Years...
Ages...

The sea plays its cold indifferent music of waves.
Eternity is still waiting for the meeting with Love.

Echo

Echo of past ages strolls along
the old narrow streets of this city.

I put my hand on the wall
that is the body of the old house.
I listen to the knocks of its heart.
It is like the clock on the wall.

Soft sure music of time…

My steps write my story
in the streets of this old city.
The Echo of my present walk will meet me
in the street tomorrow.

Two words

Two words met each other.

One of them was dressed in black.
Another word was dressed in white.
The white word was such a tender word
that it looked like a morning cloud.

And the word in black invited the white word
to live together.

"It may be such a beautiful poem
thanks to black and white colors near each other,"
the black word said.

The white word went away quietly
without any answer to the offer.

Because the white words are the words of the sky.
And the black words are the words of the earth.

The sea of oblivion

She has forgotten him.
She has put all her recollections
on the big white ship
that sailed off on the sea.
The sea of oblivion…
It is not possible to come back from that sea.
She knows it.

She has forgotten him.

But...
Only at the early morning…
Even the birds sleep…
As yet the sun is not born once again.
 She hears a ship horn sound.
The sound pierces the morning silence.

Then she closes her ears by her arms
that she could not hear it.
She whispers:
"I have forgotten you.
I have forgotten you..."

The Servants

The words are like invisible dutiful servants.

We say words to each other.
We say words in a blaze of anger.
We say words in beauty of love.

A whole host of servants…
These servants embody the words in life.

The words of hatred may become a war.
The words of love may become a baby.
The words of childlike admiration may become
an inspiration.

The invisible dutiful servants...

I heard how the sky was crying

I heard how the sky was crying.
 I was alone in my house.
The only Silence was walking in the rooms softly.
The windows were open.
The rays of the sun were slipping
above the flowers that grew before my house.
The warm day was smiling by those bright rays.

Suddenly I have heard that the sky began to cry.
The clouds were far away yet.
The rays of the sun were slipping above the flowers yet.
But the music of sadness was sounding in the calm air.
It was very close to me
and it was very far from me at the same time.

Some minutes later the clouds appeared
above my house too.
The cold drops of the rain kissed the flowers.
The rays of the sun disappeared in the air.

I heard how the sky was crying ...

Cold dew

"How do you feel?"
The sky asked clouds in the night.

"We are tired of flying along your soul,"
they answered to the sky.

"We are going to fly to the earth,"
they continued.

"It is a sad long way. You will be changed by it,"
the sky warned them.

The clouds did not listen to the words of the sky.
They were flying to the earth by drops of rain.
Flowers kissed them.
Leaves of high trees opened their green hearts to them.
The earth became wet.

"How do you feel?"
The sky asked the clouds in the early morning.
And many new little flowers laughed at this question
by the beautiful cold dew.

Four letters

The word Love was separated into four letters.

But

L - became the wings of the wind.
O - became the soul of the dream.
V - was put on the brightest star in the sky.
E - became the song of the huge free sea.

And the wind was flying
in the big soul of colored dream
where the brightest star was illuminating the song
of the huge free sea.

The letters became the word LOVE again.

The Wind

The Wind was going along the Earth's surface.
He had a long beautiful scarf.
He was dressed in the long gray coat.

The Wind was going and
the grass was leaning before him.

He was beating at the shutters of the windows.
And people were closing the windows at night.

Even proud trees were stooping down their branches
before the Wind.

People thought that the Wind was in a bad mood.
People thought that the Wind was angry.

But the Wind was going without noticing anything.
The wind was in a mighty hurry.
He knew
that the ships were already in the sea.
And the sails were waiting for his proud and
strong breath of freedom.

Beautiful child

Perhaps the wind was mixed with aroma of the night
when you was born.

The beautiful colors
of your previous lives were put inside your soul that
you could use them during your new life on the earth.

Perhaps rain mixed music of drops
with rays of the warm sun when you were born.

You opened the eyes.

The Flying wind recognized you,
"I will send you my pictures with clouds soon,
My beautiful child of this planet."

Love

The whisper of the morning mist -
I love you.

The wind with wings of night stars -
I love you.

The ship of dreams in the ocean of the night -
I love you.

And the sails of your embrace -
Love.

Transparent air of recollections

Autumn thoughts…
Autumn words..
Autumn rain.

Who put
the transparent air of recollections here?

Autumn thoughts…
Autumn words..
Autumn rain.

The crowd

A crowd of people is a crowd where a personality is lost.
The crowd of people is like a big crazy animal.
People feel more sureness together.

The personality is lost.

It is so easy to rule the animal if the personality is lost.
The crowd makes its huge steps in the streets.
The planet is falling in darkness if the personality is lost.

Contents

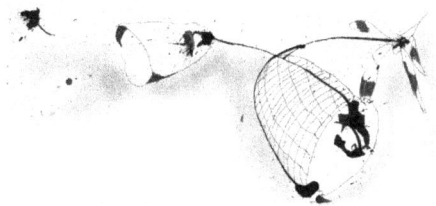

www.ingramcontent.com/pod-product-compliance
Lightning Source LLC
Chambersburg PA
CBHW060653030426
42337CB00017B/2593

9788494455902